597.92 BLO

Blomquist, Christopher

Desert tortoises

The Library of
Turtles and Tortoises™

Desert Tortoises

Christopher Blomquist

The Rosen Publishing Group's
PowerKids Press™
New York

For Carolyn, a friend to kith and creatures

Published in 2004 by The Rosen Publishing Group, Inc.
29 East 21st Street, New York, NY 10010

First Edition

Editor: Natashya Wilson
Book Design: Michael J. Caroleo
Photo Research: Michael J. Caroleo

Photo Credits: Cover and title page, p. 8 © Jonathan Blair/CORBIS; p. 4 @ CORBIS/Life in the Wild, Royalty Free CD; p. 7 © Index Stock Imagery, Inc.; p. 11 © David A. Northcot/CORBIS; p. 12 © Ted Levin/CORBIS; p. 15 © Kennan Ward/CORBIS; p. 16 by Dennis Sheridan; p. 19 © Robert Holmes/CORBIS; p. 20 © Craig Aurness/CORBIS.

Blomquist, Christopher.
Desert tortoises / Christopher Blomquist.
    v. cm. — (The library of turtles and tortoises)
Includes bibliographical references (p.).
Contents: An ancient desert dweller — The slow and steady tortoise — Female or male? — Beat the heat — Eating and drinking — Mating and nesting — Desert babies — The big sleep — Be careful out there! — Helping human hands.
ISBN 0-8239-6739-5 (lib. bdg.)
1. Desert tortoise—Juvenile literature. [1. Desert tortoise. 2. Turtles. 3. Endangered species.] I. Title. II. Series.
QL666.C584 B659 2004
597.92'4—dc21

2002155949

Manufactured in the United States of America

Contents

Carapace

Scutes

Plastron

An Ancient Desert Dweller

For more than 10,000 years the desert tortoise has made its home in what is now the dry, hot desert of the southwestern United States. Art carved into rocks by ancient peoples includes drawings of these tortoises. The pictures, along with tools and rattles made from tortoise shells and bones, show that desert tortoises have changed very little during all that time.

As do all tortoises, a desert tortoise has a hard shell that covers its body. The upper part, or **carapace**, of a desert tortoise's shell is bowl shaped and is covered in black, brown, or tan horny plates called **scutes**. The bottom, or **plastron**, of a desert tortoise's shell is yellow. The shells of most adults are from 9 to 14 ½ inches (23–37 cm) long.

A desert tortoise has broad, flat front legs. The legs' shovel-like shape helps the tortoise to dig its home. Inset: The orange area on the map shows where desert tortoises live in the United States.

The Slow and Steady Tortoise

In a story from Aesop's *Fables* titled "The Hare and the Tortoise," a slow, steady tortoise beats a fast-but-lazy hare in a race. The tale is make-believe, but one part of it is true. Tortoises are very slow! Desert tortoises walk from 1/10 to 3/10 mile per hour (0.2–0.5 km/h). A desert tortoise can take from 3 to 8 hours to move 1 mile (1.6 km). Humans can walk that distance in about 20 minutes.

Most people know they move faster than tortoises, but many don't know exactly what a tortoise is. Tortoises are turtles that live only on land and go to water only to drink or to bathe. Scientists say that tortoises are those turtles whose hind feet are shaped like an elephant's. All tortoises have high, dome-shaped shells. Other turtles may have flatter shells and webbed feet. Some turtles have soft shells!

The back legs on a desert tortoise are round with flat bottoms, as are an elephant's legs.

Gular
Horn

Female or Male?

There are about 270 different turtle species. In many species, it is hard to tell males and females apart. This is not the case with desert tortoises. Once these animals are about 8 inches (20.3 cm) long, or from 5 to 15 years old, males and females begin to look different. Females have flat plastrons and short tails. Males have dented plastrons and longer tails. Desert tortoises also have a **gular horn**, which sticks out under the chin. A female's gular horn is shorter than a male's. The male's gular horn curves upward. Every desert tortoise has a home range that it stays in and knows. Male desert tortoises usually have larger home ranges than do females, up to 1 square mile (2.6 sq km). Tortoise ranges often overlap. When two males meet, they may fight. Females are not known to fight.

The long gular horn of this male desert tortoise tilts up at the ends. Males use their gular horns to fight other males.

Beat the Heat

A desert tortoise's home range is hot and dry in the summer. Tortoises are **reptiles**. Reptiles are cold-blooded, which means their body **temperature** goes up or down with the air temperature. When the air temperature rises above 90°F (32.2°C), desert tortoises cool off by staying in holes called **burrows** that they have dug underground. The temperature and moisture inside the burrows do not change much, creating comfortable **microhabitats** for tortoises. A tortoise may have several burrows in its home range. The burrows are from 3 to 30 feet (1–9.1 m) in length. Desert tortoises often **estivate**, or become less active, inside their burrows from June until August. They stay inside for days or weeks at a time. They come out when the air is cool, usually in the morning, in the evening, or after a storm.

Staying in the shade helps desert tortoises to live in the hot, dusty desert. This tortoise is resting in its burrow.

Turtle and Tortoise Facts

Once it is in its burrow, a desert tortoise is very hard to remove. It will brace its feet against the sides and raise its back to the roof to avoid being pulled out.

Turtle and Tortoise Facts

Desert tortoises dig holes in the ground to collect rainwater.

Eating and Drinking

Adult desert tortoises are **herbivores**, or plant-eating animals. They usually eat in the morning and the evening. They will often seek out their favorite plants even if other plants are closer. In the spring, when desert flowers bloom, the tortoises eat many different types of wildflowers. They eat desert dandelions, forget-me-nots, and cactus flowers as well as fresh, green desert grasses. In the summer, many desert plants dry up. The tortoises then eat the dried plants. Young desert tortoises also eat insects, dead lizards, pieces of bone, and **dung**.

Desert tortoises get most of their water from the plants they eat. They also drink freshwater when they find it. A tortoise's body can store water for several weeks. The tortoise's body reuses the water instead of **excreting** it right away.

Cacti are a common meal for desert tortoises. This desert tortoise is dining on a beavertail cactus.

13

Mating and Nesting

Most desert tortoises start to have babies between the ages of 15 and 20. Desert tortoises **mate** when they are most active, in the spring and fall. Tortoises seek out each other's company when they are ready to mate. To court the female, the male bobs his head at her. Then he may walk around her and nibble on her nose, legs, and shell. He may also bump her with his gular horn.

After mating, females dig their nests about 6 inches (15.2 cm) deep, often near their burrows. It takes a female from 1 to 5 hours to dig a nest, lay her eggs, and bury them. She uses her hind legs to dig the nest, place the eggs in it, and cover it up. Desert tortoises lay anywhere from 2 to 15 round, hard-shelled, white eggs. Some females lay from two to three **clutches** of eggs in one mating season.

This female desert tortoise is big enough to have babies. The younger, smaller desert tortoises probably are not.

Turtle and Tortoise Facts

To soften the ground for digging a nest, a female will sometimes urinate, or release liquid waste from her body, onto the dirt. The smell may help to keep enemies away from the nest.

Turtle and Tortoise Facts

Hatchlings are much less friendly than adults. They hiss and bite when touched by humans. Adults are usually very calm.

Desert Babies

Once a female tortoise buries her eggs, her mothering duties are done. She does not take care of the nest or the babies, which are called **hatchlings**. They must fend for themselves. Depending on the temperature of the nest, the eggs usually take from 90 to 120 days to hatch. Often, some eggs in a clutch will hatch sooner than others. Sometimes an egg produces twin tortoises! Newborn desert tortoises are from 1 $\frac{2}{5}$ to 1 $\frac{4}{5}$ inches (36–48 mm) long. Their shells are soft and are about as thick as a person's fingernail. The shells will not fully harden for at least five years. Then the bones beneath the scutes begin to grow and thicken. The hatchlings' soft shells and small size make them easy food for ravens and other **predators**.

This desert tortoise hatchling has just broken out of its egg. Only from 1 to 5 hatchlings per 100 will live to adulthood.

Sleeping Through the Winter

Turtles stay inside when the weather is very hot. However, they also stay in when the weather turns cold. In October, when temperatures in the desert are from 40°F to 60°F (4.4°C–15.6°C), desert tortoises will **hibernate**, or go to sleep for the winter. They go into their burrows and do not usually come out until spring. Wood rats and snakes sometimes share the tortoise burrows in the winter. Desert tortoises are good climbers and will often dig their hibernation burrows at the tops of steep slopes. During hibernation, a tortoise's heart rate, breathing rate, and other body systems slow down. The hibernating tortoise lives off fat that its body has stored in its legs and shoulders. Desert tortoises come out of hibernation sometime in February through April.

Desert tortoises hibernate in their burrows during the winter. Some hibernate together, in groups of as many as 23 tortoises.

Be Careful Out There!

Desert tortoises can live for more than 100 years. However, these creatures also face many dangers that can cut their lives short. Eggs and hatchlings are often eaten by animals such as coyotes, badgers, eagles, roadrunners, and ravens. Coyotes and kit foxes sometimes attack adult tortoises. Tortoises will also die if they tip over and are unable to right themselves. In the wild, most tortoises do not live more than 50 years.

Humans cause the most desert tortoise deaths. The building of cities in the desert, such as Las Vegas in Nevada, has destroyed much of the desert tortoise's natural **habitat**. Tortoises are hit by cars on desert highways and are crushed in their burrows by off-road **vehicles** (ORVs). The desert tortoise is now listed as an **endangered** species.

Cars can hit desert tortoises when they walk onto roads. The tortoises move too slowly to get out of the way.

Helping Human Hands

People and governments are working hard to make sure that the desert tortoise doesn't die out forever. Today tens of thousands of desert tortoises are bred by people to be kept as pets. In California, desert tortoises can be kept as pets. A pet tortoise must be licensed. When given the proper care, pet desert tortoises usually live much longer, healthier lives than do their relatives in the wild.

Refuges give wild tortoises a safe place to live and breed. The 39-square-mile (101-sq-km) Desert Tortoise Natural Area refuge in California was founded in 1973. It does not permit ORVs within its borders. Although humans have been the desert tortoise's worst enemy, they may also be this special animal's only hope for living in the future.

Glossary

burrows (BUR-ohz) Holes that animals dig in the ground.

carapace (KER-uh-pays) The upper part of a turtle's shell.

clutches (KLUCH-ez) Groups of eggs laid by female animals at one time.

dung (DUNG) Animal waste.

endangered (en-DAYN-jerd) In danger of no longer existing.

estivate (ES-tih-vayt) To spend the summer resting.

excreting (eks-KREET-ing) Getting rid of, passing through the body.

gular horn (GYOO-ler HORN) A hornlike piece of a tortoise's shell that sticks out below the throat.

habitat (HA-bih-tat) The surroundings where an animal or a plant naturally lives.

hatchlings (HACH-lingz) Baby animals that have just come out of their eggshells.

herbivores (ER-bih-vorz) Animals that eat plants.

hibernate (HY-bur-nayt) To spend the winter in a sleeplike state.

mate (MAYT) To join together to make babies.

microhabitats (my-kroh-HA-bih-tats) Small areas, in which animals live, that are different from their outer surroundings.

plastron (PLAS-tron) The bottom, flatter part of a tortoise's shell that covers the belly.

predators (PREH-duh-terz) Animals that kill other animals for food.

refuges (REH-fyooj-ez) Places that give shelter or security.

reptiles (REP-tylz) Cold-blooded animals with lungs and scales.

scutes (SKOOTS) Hard, bony plates or large scales.

species (SPEE-sheez) A single kind of living thing.

temperature (TEM-pruh-chur) How hot or cold something is.

vehicles (VEE-uh-kulz) Means of moving or carrying things.

Index

A
Aesop, 6

B
burrows, 10, 18

C
carapace, 5
clutches, 14

D
Desert Tortoise Natural
    Area, 22

E
eggs, 14, 17, 21

G
gular horn, 9, 14

H
"Hare and the Tortoise,
    The," 6
hatchlings, 17, 21
herbivores, 13
hibernate, 18
home range, 9–10

I
Ice Age, 5

M
mate, 14
microhabitats, 10

O
off-road vehicles
    (ORVs), 21–22

P
plastron(s), 5, 9
predators, 17

S
scutes, 5

Web Sites

Due to the changing nature of Internet links, PowerKids Press has developed an online list of Web sites related to the subject of this book. This site is updated regularly. Please use this link to access the list:
www.powerkidslinks.com/ltt/desert/